Surviving and Thriving: 365 Days in Lagos

Sunil Kumar

Published by Sunil Kumar, 2024.

SURVIVING AND THRIVING: 365 DAYS IN LAGOS

First edition. October 2, 2024.

Copyright © 2024 Sunil Kumar.

ISBN: 979-8227220462

Written by Sunil Kumar.

Table of Contents

Introduction

———

Have you ever caught yourself daydreaming about life in one of the world's most dynamic and populous cities? Imagine, for a moment, standing on the bustling streets of Lagos, Nigeria—a megacity teeming with relentless energy, vibrant culture, and unparalleled diversity. You hear the melodic chatter of traders in the market, the rhythmic beats of Afrobeat music drifting through the air, and the hum of activity that never seems to rest. Welcome to Lagos, a city that defies simple definitions and invites you to lose yourself in its ceaseless motion.

Lagos is often described as the heartbeat of Nigeria, the economic nerve center that propels the national economy forward. With a population surpassing 20 million people, it is not just a city but a living, breathing organism with a unique rhythm and character. The purpose of this book is to offer you a comprehensive exploration of life in Lagos, from the moment you step off the plane at Murtala Muhammed International Airport to the time you weave through its complex streets, savor its diverse cuisine, and navigate its myriad challenges. This book is your personal guide, combining practical advice, rich cultural insights, and heartfelt anecdotes to help you understand what it truly means to live in this extraordinary megacity.

What sets this book apart is its blend of factual information and personal experiences, making it not only an informative read but also an engaging journey through the streets and alleys of Lagos. Unlike travel brochures or academic texts that often paint either an overly romanticized or excessively critical picture, this book aims to provide a balanced, nuanced view that highlights both the challenges and rewards of life in this vibrant urban environment.

Among the key themes explored in this book is the initial culture shock that almost every newcomer experiences upon arrival. Lagos is a sensory overload—its sights, sounds, and smells can be overwhelming but also incredibly captivating. Whether you're navigating the chaotic traffic, engaging with local vendors in the markets, or adapting to the spicy flavors of local cuisine, every aspect of daily life offers a new challenge and an opportunity for growth.

Another critical theme is the intricate social dynamics and the importance of building relationships. Lagos is a city where who you know can significantly impact your experience. Learning the art of bargaining in markets, forging connections with locals and expatriates, and navigating the cultural nuances in social settings are all essential skills for thriving in this megacity.

The book also delves into the practical aspects of settling down—finding housing, dealing with frequent power outages, and coping with water scarcity. These are not mere inconveniences but critical issues that shape everyday life. Understanding how to manage these challenges can make the difference between merely surviving and truly thriving in Lagos.

Additionally, the city's rich cultural tapestry is another focal point. From its diverse religious practices to its booming arts scene, encompassing Nollywood films and contemporary art galleries, Lagos offers a cultural smorgasbord that is as enriching as it is diverse. The role of language, specifically the use of Pidgin English and local slang, adds another layer to the social fabric, providing both opportunities for deeper connection and potential misunderstandings.

This book is particularly relevant for anyone considering a move to Lagos, whether for work, study, or other reasons. It is also invaluable for expatriates who have recently arrived and are in the process of adjusting to their new environment. Even for those who have lived in Lagos for a while, this book offers fresh perspectives and insights that can enhance their understanding and appreciation of the city.

By the time you finish reading, you will have gained a treasure trove of new knowledge and skills—from negotiating with landlords and understanding the local economy to appreciating the complexities of the informal sector and navigating the city's nightlife safely. You will also gain a deeper appreciation for the resilience and ingenuity of Lagos's residents, who continuously adapt to the city's ever-changing landscape.

So, buckle up for an unforgettable journey through one of Africa's largest and most vibrant cities. Let this book be your compass as you navigate the exhilarating, often perplexing, but ultimately rewarding experience of life in Lagos. The pages ahead promise to not only inform but also inspire, as you explore the complexities, joys, and challenges that define life in this remarkable megacity.

Chapter 1 Welcome to Lagos

Lagos, Nigeria's most populous city with a populationing 20 million, is a sprawling megacity characterized by a frenetic energy and a relentless pace of life. An initial introduction to this seemingly chaotic urban environment is both exhilarating and daunting. First impressions of Lagos paint a sensory tapestry that is rich and overwhelming, providing an immersive initiation for any new arrival.

Arrival at Murtala Muhammed International Airport

The journey begins as soon as you set foot in Murtala Muhammed International Airport, the primary gateway to Lagos. This bustling airport, named after Nigeria's former military ruler, is a microcosm of the city itself. The first encounter with the undulating crowd, the cacophony of voices speaking a symphony of languages, and the blending scents of the tropics with the urban undercurrent of petrol and commerce signals the start of a unique adventure.

The airport experience is a rite of passage. From the jostling baggage claim area to the somewhat chaotic customs stations, the pressure of navigating this space feels immediate. Yet, amidst the frenzy, there are pockets of understanding and efficiency. The seasoned travelers move with a discernible rhythm, knowing exactly how to navigate the ebb and flow of the crowd, reflecting the adaptive spirit that one needs to thrive in Lagos.

Sensory Overload: Sights, Sounds, and Smells

Exiting the airport, the sensory overload continues—in vivid, multifaceted ways. The sights are the first to hit. A mosaic of color dominates the landscape. Yellow danfos (mini-buses) hurtle through the streets, often laden with passengers and splashes of vibrant paint. The architecture tells many stories, from modern skyscrapers to the densely packed, lively neighborhoods. Billboards and hand-painted signs compete in a visual symphony, advertising everything from mobile services to local delicacies.

The sounds of Lagos form an ever-present backdrop: the constant hum of traffic punctuated by car horns blaring in a staccato rhythm, the loud and infectious calls of street vendors, music pouring out of tiny shops and eateries, merging into an eclectic soundtrack that mirrors the city's diversity. These sounds create a pulse that underlines the vivacity of Lagos.

Equally potent are the smells, a confluence of urban and coastal scents. The briny scent of the Atlantic Ocean mingles with the pungent aroma of street foods—roasting corn, spiced meats, and freshly fried plantains. Mixed in are the less pleasant, but no less defining, scents of open gutters and petrochemical exhaust, painting a realistic olfactory picture of this urban behemoth.

Initial Culture Shock and Adjustment

For newcomers, this sensory richness can trigger an intense culture shock. The immediate reaction often includes a mix of awe and discomfort, a recognition of both the beauty and challenges inherent in this new environment. Lagos commands a level of stamina and resilience, testing even the most prepared individuals.

Adjusting to the pace of Lagos requires an acceptance of its inherent contradictions and an ability to adapt to its rhythms. For many, the initial days blur into a whirlwind of navigation—both literal and figurative. Finding one's bearings among the crowded streets and understanding the unspoken rules of social conduct can be daunting. However, in the midst of this maelstrom, there are revealing moments of connection and discovery.

Integration into Lagosian life often begins with building a foundational understanding of its social framework. Initial steps might involve seeking advice from locals, other expatriates, or long-term residents who offer invaluable navigational tips and cultural insights. Learning to greet people in Yoruba or Hausa, the dominant local languages, elicits smiles and establishes a bridge between cultures, serving as an early key to unlocking Lagosian hospitality, which, as it turns out, is boundless and generous.

Importantly, understanding that initial discomfort is a normal part of the transition process helps. Through shared experiences in forums, expatriate groups, or conversations with neighbors, one finds a communal sense of resilience. This shared understanding fosters inclusivity, easing the psychological transition from outsider to participant in the life of the city.

In this initial phase, embracing flexibility and openness is crucial. Lagos challenges preconceived notions and forces you to broaden your perspectives. The very culture shock that at first feels overwhelming can transform into a riveting engagement with a city that, while seemingly chaotic, operates on its own unique logic and rhythm.

Through patient adaptation and a willingness to navigate its ebbs and flows, Lagos reveals itself as a city of immense depth and possibility. The sensory challenges of those first few days gradually become the rich, colored threads of daily life, woven into an intricate tapestry of experiences that define one's journey in this

extraordinary metropolitan landscape.

Chapter 2: Finding a Home in the Chaos

———

Arriving in Lagos, Nigeria's bustling megacity, is often accompanied an initial wave of excitement and trepidation. Yet, once the first impressions settle, the paramount task at hand becomes finding a place to call home amidst the chaos. This chapter delves into the labyrinthine process of securing housing, negotiating with landlords, setting up essential utilities, and ultimately creating a sanctuary in the heart of the urban sprawl.

House Hunting in Different Neighborhoods

Navigating the myriad of neighborhoods in Lagos can feel overwhelming, each area with its distinct atmosphere and amenities. From the upscale, tranquil streets of Ikoyi to the pulsating energy of Surulere, the choice of neighborhood is pivotal in shaping one's Lagos experience. Ikoyi, known for its affluent residents and gated communities, offers a respite from the city's frenetic pace, boasting tree-lined streets and impressive mansions. In contrast, Surulere, with its buzzing street life and more affordable housing options, presents a vivid snapshot of Lagosian living.

Lekki Peninsula serves as another popular choice, especially among expatriates and middle-income families. Known for its modern architecture and burgeoning commercial hubs, Lekki combines the essence of upscale living with accessibility to beaches, restaurants, and shops. Victoria Island stands as the commercial heart of the city, appealing to those who appreciate both residential comfort and proximity to business districts. The island sparkles with posh apartments, luxurious hotels, and a vibrant nightlife, being a glaring example of urban sophistication.

However, house hunting in Lagos is seldom straightforward. Potential home seekers often find themselves navigating myriad challenges, including fluctuating rental prices, varying levels of housing quality, and the omnipresent traffic that can turn what appears to be a short commute into an odyssey. The need to find a balance between budget constraints and personal preferences often becomes the central theme of the search.

Negotiating with Landlords and Agents

Once a suitable neighborhood has been identified, the next step involves engaging with landlords and real estate agents—this engagement often comes with its nuances and occasional frustrations. It is common for prospective tenants to encounter layers of bureaucracy and, perhaps more dauntingly, the art of negotiation.

In Lagos, the rental process is highly fluid and requires a certain level of shrewdness. Unlike many Western countries where rental prices are often fixed, here they serve as starting points for negotiation. To navigate these waters efficiently, one must be prepared for a certain degree of bargaining. Skilled agents and landlords often anticipate haggling, having factored such negotiations into the initial asking price. Therefore, engaging in the bargaining process becomes not merely an option but a necessity. Prospective renters benefit substantially from partnering with local agents who possess a deep understanding of market values and cultural nuances, even as they facilitate interactions with landlords.

A recurring challenge is the concept of "agency fees" and "agreement fees," often equating to a significant percentage of the annual rental cost. These fees, while typical in the Nigerian context, can sometimes catch expatriates or new residents off guard, who might be unaccustomed to such additional costs. Effective negotiation may involve not only the base rental price but also these associated fees, striving to reach a mutually agreeable settlement.

Setting Up Utilities and Essential Services

Securing a home in Lagos signifies merely the commencement of another arduous journey: setting up utilities and essential services. The challenges faced here can be multifaceted, compounded by issues such as irregular service delivery and bureaucratic inefficiency. However, understanding and preparing for these challenges can mitigate the stress involved.

Electricity supply in Lagos is notoriously unreliable. Frequent power outages, colloquially known as "NEPA" or more recently "PHCN" issues (named after the once government-owned electricity company), mean that owning a generator is as essential as securing a lease. Setting up electricity involves registering with the power company, ensuring that meter reading is accurate, and often prepaying for electricity through recharge units.

Similarly, water supply isn't always straightforward. While some apartments come equipped with boreholes that guarantee a steady water supply, others rely on less consistent sources. Setting up a dependable source of water may necessitate engaging a local service for periodic water delivery. Ensuring water quality also often requires installing filtration systems, especially in households with sensitive members or those wary of local waterborne diseases.

Moreover, internet connectivity represents a critical aspect of modern living and working. Fortunately, Lagos has witnessed substantial strides in this regard, with various providers offering competitive packages. Navigating these options, however, demands patience and diligence to find a reliable service that ensures consistency and adequate speed. Some residents opt for mobile internet solutions as backups to mitigate unforeseen service downtimes from fixed-line providers.

Creating a Sanctuary Amidst the Urban Sprawl

In a city as fast-paced and incessantly active as Lagos, transforming one's living space into a sanctuary is pivotal for mental and emotional well-being. The concept of home takes on profound significance, serving as a refuge from the relentless hustle.

When it comes to furnishing and decorating, Lagos offers an eclectic mix of options ranging from high-end furniture stores in Victoria Island to bustling markets like Alaba International Market, renowned for its affordable and diverse selection. Blending personal tastes with local influences often results in a unique and comforting home environment. Adorning spaces with locally sourced art and crafts not only enhances aesthetics but also provides economic support to local artisans.

However, the essence of creating a sanctuary extends beyond decor. Given the frequent power outages, ensuring reliable power supply through generators or inverters becomes crucial. Likewise, adopting measures to reduce noise intrusion—whether through heavy curtains, soundproofing, or simply strategic room arrangements—can significantly enhance tranquility.

In Lagos, security remains a fundamental concern and a vital component of one's sanctuary. Most apartments come with essential security features such as gates and guards, but additional measures like reinforced doors, surveillance cameras, and security systems can provide peace of mind. Establishing a good relationship with neighbors and community security personnel can also contribute to a safer living environment.

Creating a home in Lagos is a multifaceted endeavor that involves not only selection and negotiation but also adaptation and preparation. The journey, strewn with challenges, ultimately provides an invaluable opportunity for growth and immersion into the dynamic fabric of this captivating city. As the process unfolds, newcomers find themselves transitioning from initial bewilderment to a deep, albeit complex, appreciation of Lagos—its vibrancy, resilience, and unyielding spirit.

Chapter 3: Navigating the Lagos Maze

Navigating Lagos an art form, a crucial skill that must be mastered by anyone wishes to thrive in this frenetic city. While the vast, sprawling metropolis can initially seem bewildering, filled with labyrinthine roads teeming with chaotic traffic, learning how to traverse its maze is an essential part of integrating into Lagos life. The journey to understanding Lagos traffic and its myriad nuances begins with the recognition that the city's lifeline is its congested roads, a web of connections sustaining the pulse of the nation's largest urban center.

Introduction to Lagos Traffic and Road Systems

First, one must embrace the reality of Lagos traffic. The seemingly endless flow of vehicles — from the diminutive "keke" tricycles to the hulking articulated lorries — all jostling for supremacy on roads that frequently morph from tarmacked highways into rugged dirt tracks. Lagos traffic is infamous for its unpredictability; a short 10-kilometer journey can take anywhere from 15 minutes to three hours, depending on the time of day, route taken, and sheer luck.

Navigating these roads requires a sound understanding of their structure and the unspoken rules that govern them. Lagos is divided into mainland and island sectors, each with distinct characteristics. The Third Mainland Bridge, one of the longest in Africa, serves as the primary connector between the two. The mainland boasts densely populated residential areas like Ikeja and Surulere while the island is home to commercial districts such as Victoria Island and

Lekki. Locales such as Ikorodu and Epe, farther-flung but increasingly significant, complete the labyrinth.

Knowing the major arterial roads, such as Ikorodu Road, Lagos-Badagry Expressway, and Lekki-Epe Expressway, is essential. These roads branch out into smaller avenues and streets (often unnamed on official maps but bustling with life and commerce) that weave through the city like veins. Notably, the roads often have checkpoints manned by police or local authorities, ostensibly for security but also offering entrepreneurial opportunities, as interactions at these points can often involve some level of negotiation or "settlement."

Learning to Use Various Modes of Transportation

Understanding the road system, however, is only half the battle. The other half involves mastering the various modes of transportation that ply these roads. Choices abound: private cars, public buses, taxis, motorcycles, and tricycles, each with its own pros and cons.

Private vehicles offer the most comfort and flexibility but come with the challenge of finding parking in the congested city. Moreover, the cost of fuel and the need for a reliable mechanic cannot be understated. Public buses, primarily the iconic yellow "danfos," are the heartbeat of Lagos public transportation. Typically seating 14 to 18 passengers, these buses operate on a semi-fixed route system, their destinations often hollered out by a conductor who doubles as the fare collector. While cheap and ubiquitous, danfos can be distressingly unreliable and uncomfortably crowded.

For shorter trips, "okadas" (motorcycle taxis) provide a quick, albeit sometimes perilous, way to navigate traffic.

Their agility allows them to weave through gridlocked cars, significantly reducing travel time during peak hours. These are less formal than buses and require some degree of bargaining skill to secure a fair fare. Tricycles, known locally as "kekes," offer a middle ground between the chaos of motorcycles and the structure of buses. They are a popular choice in mainland areas where roads are narrower.

Taxis offer more comfort and privacy than buses and motorcycle taxis, appearing in various forms across the city. Traditional taxis, painted yellow or black depending on the area, can be flagged down on the street or found at designated taxi parks. While these taxis run on negotiated fares, more structured services like Uber and Bolt provide an alternative with set prices and a ratings system — a welcome feature for foreigners and locals alike who seek reliability.

Encounters with "Danfo" Buses and Motorcycle Taxis

Experiences with danfo buses and okadas are central to understanding the DNA of Lagos. The danfo is communal by nature. Passengers share not just the vehicle but also the highs and lows of transit life: the sudden nap of a fellow passenger who inadvertently uses your shoulder as a pillow, the comedic banter between driver and conductor, and the shared grumbling when traffic grinds to a halt. Commuters establish silent pacts of endurance, camaraderie amid the clamor.

Motorcycle taxis, on the other hand, are where the dance with danger becomes evident. Speeding through narrow streets, okadas defy conventional rules of the road. Held on tightly as these wheeled saviors cut through jams, passengers gain the full sensory experience of Lagos. The wind in one's face, the close-up views of street vendors, the sudden lurch as the driver avoids a pothole or an oncoming vehicle — it's adrenaline, practicality, and survival rolled into one.

Using motorcycles also means understanding the inherent risks. Lagos roads can be treacherous, and accidents involving okadas are far from rare. Yet, many residents and even expatriates find the efficiency they offer indispensable. For many, the seemingly reckless navigation of okada drivers is often tempered by a peculiar kind of professionalism — an intimate knowledge of shortcuts, traffic patterns, and the quirks of the urban terrain that seasoned riders rely upon.

Developing Strategies for Efficient Commuting

Efficiency in commuting across Lagos involves more than just knowing the modes of transport and the road networks. It requires a nuanced strategy, almost a ritual that involves planning, flexibility, and a keen sense of timing.

One fundamental strategy is to travel outside peak hours whenever possible. The traditional rush hours of 6-9 AM and 4-7 PM see the worst traffic, transforming what should be quick trips into endurance tests. Planning meetings and errands around these times can save considerable time and stress. For instance, night commuting, while fraught with its risks, offers the benefit of clearer roads and faster travel times.

Another critical aspect is the use of technology. Traffic apps like Google Maps, combined with local knowledge from apps like Gidi Traffic, offer real-time updates on congestion, accidents, and road blockages. Advanced route planning using these tools ensures that one avoids the most notorious traffic black spots. Additionally, "group taxi-hailing" apps

Rideshare services like Uber or Bolt have also found their niches among those who prefer a middle ground between public and private transport.

Flexibility remains paramount. Routes that work one day might be clogged the next. Experienced commuters often have backup routes and alternative transportation modes in mind, switching between danfo, okada, and keke as the situation dictates. For many, this adaptability extends to a psychological readiness to deal with delays, the unplanned, and the unusual — a state of zen-like acceptance of the traffic gods' whims.

Fueling oneself is another practical strategy; keeping snacks and water handy can help maintain energy during prolonged stints in traffic. Additionally, cultivating the habit of carrying small denominations in cash eases transactions with conductors, okada riders, and vendors for those quick roadside purchases, something particularly crucial in a city where digital payments, while growing, are not always reliable.

Ultimately, navigating Lagos is an acquired skill, one that blends knowledge with intuition, and local wisdom with personal experience. Every journey, every interaction, becomes part of a larger understanding, a weaving of one's own path into the complex, ever-shifting tapestry that is Lagos. As one learns to navigate the city's maze, one also learns to appreciate the rhythm of this dynamic urban environment, discovering that within the chaos lies a unique and vibrant order.

Chapter 4: The Art of Bargaining

In Lagos, markets are more than just places to buy; they are bustling ecosystems teeming with life, a microcosm of the city's vibrancy. Each market in Lagos offers a unique flavor, from the sprawling Balogun Market on Lagos Island to the more compact and specialized Lekki Arts and Crafts Market. Understanding the dance of commerce in these markets is essential, and one must become proficient in the art of bargaining to navigate them successfully. It's a skill that goes beyond mere price negotiation—it involves understanding the cultural nuances and forming connections that may offer long-term benefits.

Introduction to Lagos Markets

Walking through a Lagos market for the first time can be both exhilarating and overwhelming. The sensory experience is intense: the vivid colors of fabric stalls, the varied textures of raw foodstuff, the aromatic spices, and the cacophony of sounds made by traders hawking their wares. These markets are a vivid representation of Lagos life—chaotic yet organized, bustling yet intimate. Major markets like Balogun, Tejuosho, and Mile 12 are hubs of activity where traders and customers come together in a daily ritual that is as much about social interaction as it is about commerce.

One of the most striking observations is the sheer diversity of goods available. From imported electronics and designer knock-offs to locally produced goods and fresh produce, there is little that cannot be found in Lagos markets. Each trader has carved out a niche, and understanding where to find what you need is a journey of discovery and interaction. The structural setup of markets in Lagos often seems chaotic, but there is a method to the madness—certain sections of the market are designated for specific types of goods, and knowing these unwritten rules saves time and effort.

Learning the Etiquette of Haggling

Haggling, or bargaining, is an art form in Lagos, deeply ingrained in the culture and expected in almost every transaction. It goes beyond simply negotiating the price; it is a social interaction, a performance, and often a test of wits. The etiquette of haggling in Lagos requires one to be polite yet firm, friendly yet persuasive. It's a delicate balance that can be perfected with time and practice.

The process typically begins with the trader quoting a price that is significantly higher than the expected final sale price. This is where the buyer's skill comes into play. It's common practice to counter with an offer that is substantially lower than what one is actually willing to pay. This initiates a back-and-forth exchange, often accompanied by lively banter and expressions of disbelief at the opposing party's audacity.

Successful haggling relies heavily on reading the situation and understanding the nuances of communication. Non-verbal cues such as body language and facial expressions can often reveal how far a trader is willing to drop the price. Patience is a virtue here—rushing the process is a common mistake that can result in paying more than necessary. Moreover, showing respect for the trader's craft and their time can make a significant difference. Building a rapport often leads to more favorable deals, and repeat visits to the same vendors can foster relationships that benefit both parties.

Building Relationships with Local Vendors

The importance of building relationships with vendors cannot be overstated. In Lagos, repeat business is highly valued, and establishing a strong rapport with a vendor can lead to numerous advantages, including better prices, exclusive deals, and high-quality goods. Trust is a key currency in these interactions, much like in any other close-knit community.

To foster these relationships, it helps to show genuine interest in the lives and products of the vendors. Taking the time to ask about the origins of their goods, the challenges they face, or even their personal stories can break down barriers. These interactions often go beyond the transactional and offer a deeper connection that can be mutually beneficial. Vendors who feel valued and respected are more likely to go the extra mile to ensure customer satisfaction, whether that means holding onto an item, offering a discount, or providing insight into market trends.

Regularly patronizing the same stalls also signals loyalty, which is often reciprocated. In some cases, you might find that a trusted vendor will inform you about the best times to shop for deals, the arrival of new stock, or even market days when rare goods are available. This insider knowledge can be invaluable in navigating the bustling market landscape of Lagos.

Discovering Hidden Gems in the Bustling Marketplaces

Beyond the surface chaos of Lagos markets lies a multitude of hidden gems waiting to be discovered. These treasures are often found through exploration and interaction—whether it's an obscure stall selling artisanal crafts, a trader with a unique collection of vintage clothing, or a food vendor known only to locals for their exceptional flavors. The key to finding these hidden gems lies in the willingness to venture off the beaten path and engage deeply with the market environment.

For example, the Lekki Arts and Crafts Market is a paradise for those interested in Nigerian art and handcrafted goods. Here, one can find intricate carvings, vibrant textiles, and jewelry that are not only aesthetically pleasing but also hold cultural significance. Similarly, Balogun Market, though known for its overwhelming size, hosts numerous small vendors who specialize in rare and high-quality African prints, sometimes offering designs that are not found elsewhere.

Sometimes, the hidden gems are not physical goods at all but unique experiences and knowledge. Traders often have fascinating stories and insights into the cultural and historical context of their products. Listening to a fabric seller recount the history of Ankara prints or a spice vendor explain traditional uses for their wares can enrich one's understanding of Nigerian culture in ways that go beyond the transactional.

In conclusion, mastering the art of bargaining in Lagos markets requires a blend of cultural understanding, social skills, and strategic savvy. It is an immersive experience that goes beyond mere shopping, offering a window into Lagosian life, relationships, and the vibrant economic ecosystem that sustains one of the most

dynamic cities in Africa. Each market visit builds upon the last, layering knowledge, connections, and experiences that collectively demystify the initial chaos, revealing the rich and intricate tapestry of Lagosian commerce and culture.

Chapter 5 Feasting on Lagos Fl

an undeniable truth that holds the power to people across cultural divides serving as a gateway understanding and appreciating new. Lagos, a city brimming diversity and vibrancy, offers a culinary landscape is as rich and varied as its population. feast on Lagos flavors to embark on a gastronomic adventure thatizes the senses and the palate in ways are both surprising and delightful.

From the moment sets foot in the city the aromas of street food invade the nostr, coaxing the uninitiated to partake what becomes a culinary rite of passage The streets are crowded vendors selling everything from yam and plantains to grilled and an array of pastries Each delicacy has a story, steeped tradition and flavored by hands that have prepared for generations.

Exploring Local Cuisine and Street Food

To understand Lagos is to understand its food, and to begin, one must explore the city's vibrant street food scene. Street food vending is not just a business in Lagos; it's an institution. The street vendors, known locally as "mama put" for the women who typically man the stalls, are as varied in their offerings as the city itself.

Suya, for instance, is a must-try for anyone new to Lagos. This spicy, skewered meat is usually prepared by street vendors from Northern Nigeria, and each bite explodes with a mix of smoky heat and rich, savory undertones. The preparation of suya is an art form, with a marinade

of ground peanuts, spices, and oil that coats each strip of meat before it hits the grill. Often enjoyed with thinly sliced onions and tomatoes, and occasionally wrapped in flatbread, suya represents the perfect harmony of spice, crunch, and juiciness.

Another street food staple is jollof rice, a dish that serves as both comfort food and celebratory fare. Almost every Nigerian household has a version of jollof rice, but Lagosian street vendors have mastered a recipe that keeps passersby coming back for more. Cooked in a rich tomato sauce with peppers, onions, and a blend of spices, and often served with fried plantains and stewed meats, jollof rice in Lagos is emblematic of the city's love for bold, hearty flavors.

Dining Etiquette and Social Norms

Eating in Lagos, whether on the streets or in a more formal setting, is intrinsically tied to social customs and norms that reflect deeply ingrained cultural values. Understanding these unwritten rules can enrich one's culinary experiences and foster a deeper connection with the local culture.

One of the first things to understand is the communal nature of meals. In many Nigerian households and eateries, sharing food is a deeply rooted practice. Plates are often passed around, and it's common for meals to be eaten family-style. It's important to appreciate and embrace this shared dining experience as it speaks to the communal ethos that permeates much of Lagos life.

Another point of etiquette pertains to the act of eating with one's hands. While utensils are commonly used, many traditional dishes are best enjoyed by using one's right hand—considered the clean and respectful hand in many African cultures. This practice is particularly relevant with dishes like pounded yam and egusi soup, where one tears off a piece of the starchy yam and uses it to scoop up the flavorful soup. The tactile engagement with food enhances the sensory experience, creating a tangible connection to the ingredients and customs.

Favorite Eateries and Food Joints

Pinned across the vast map of Lagos are eateries that have not only withstood the test of time but have also become culinary landmarks. These establishments vary widely—from high-end restaurants offering modern takes on traditional dishes to modest bukas (local canens) that capture the essence of home-cooked Nigerian food.

Among the most beloved of these is Yellow Chilli. Known for its exemplary service and innovative menu, Yellow Chilli serves Lagosian staples with a contemporary twist. The egusi soup here is a revelation—rich, textured, and brimming with flavors that exhibit a careful balance of spice and umami. The restaurant's jollof rice, meanwhile, has achieved a legendary status, often cited in glowing terms by both locals and expatriates alike.

Equally noteworthy is Bukka Hut, a chain of eateries that has made a name for itself by serving authentic Nigerian dishes at affordable prices. Here, one can savor the hearty flavors of efo riro (spinach stew) paired with succulent pieces of goat meat or the pepper soup, a fiery broth that is as invigorating as it is delicious. Bukka Hut's approach to traditional recipes ensures that the dishes are both accessible and excellently executed.

However, the real soul of Lagosian cuisine is often found in the city's innumerable roadside stalls and informal joints. A perfect example is White House, located in Yaba. Known for its draw of local artists and students, this unassuming eatery has gained a cult following for its generous portions of tasty, no-nonsense Nigerian food. Their amala and gbegiri (a combination of yam flour swallow and a bean soup) offer a comforting, deeply satisfying meal that captures the heart of Nigerian gastronomy.

Adapting to Spicy Flavors and New Ingredients

Navigating the spicy and often unfamiliar terrain of Lagosian cuisine can be daunting for the uninitiated. For many newcomers, the intensity of Nigerian spices can be an initial challenge. However, with an open mind and a bit of culinary curiosity, these vibrant flavors become not only palatable but highly addictive. Adaptation is key, and several approaches can ease this transition.

A gradual exposure to different levels of spice is often recommended. By starting with dishes that are mildly spiced and progressively venturing into those with more heat, one allows their palate to adjust without overwhelming it. For instance, beginning with jollof rice or pepper soup—which offer a balanced spice that complements their overall flavor profiles—can serve as an excellent introduction.

Additionally, understanding the ingredients commonly used in Lagos cuisine can demystify many of the dishes. Staples like cassava, yams, plantains, and beans form the base of many meals, providing hearty, starchy backdrops that pair well with the city's bolder flavors. Key spices such as ginger, garlic, and Scotch bonnet peppers create the characteristic heat, while more subtle additions like ground beans, dried fish, and locust beans add depth and complexity.

When faced with a particularly spicy dish, there are practical methods to manage the heat. Traditionally, cooling foods and drinks, such as yogurt or dairy-based beverages, can neutralize the burn. Many Lagosians also recommend pairing spicy food with batons of fresh vegetables or sips of palm wine—a sweet, fermented drink that offers a refreshing counterbalance.

In many ways, adapting to the spice-laden cuisine of Lagos is a metaphor for adapting to the city itself. There may be an initial overwhelming intensity—of flavors, of experiences, of challenges—but as one becomes acclimated, they find layers of richness and enjoyment that form a deep and lasting appreciation for this dynamic urban environment.

Transitioning seamlessly to broader aspects of daily life in Lagos, understanding the food culture provides a valuable lens through which one can comprehend the city's broader socio-cultural fabric. After all, in a place where the flavors are as diverse and complex as the people, navigating gastronomic landscapes can impart invaluable lessons about community, resilience, and the unifying power of shared experiences.

Chapter 6: The Language of Lagos

In a city as vast and multifaceted as Lagos, language is both a bridge and a barrier, a tool that connects and sometimes divides. Navigating the linguistic landscape is a quintessential part of becoming acclimated to life in this bustling megacity. Here, language evolves not as a static set of rules and vocabulary but as a living, breathing entity that adapts to the rhythm and flow of daily life. From formal English to Pidgin, from Yoruba nuances to the mixed vernacular of the streets, communication in Lagos is as dynamic and varied as its people.

In Lagos, English is the official language, used in government documents, business transactions, and educational institutions. Yet, stepping out into the streets, you encounter the pulsating heartbeat of the city's linguistic diversity. Conversations blend English with Pidgin, peppered with Yoruba, Igbo, and Hausa phrases, making the art of communication a multifaceted challenge for newcomers.

Navigating the Linguistic Landscape

Walking through Lagos, one quickly notices that language here is more a tapestry than a monolith. English serves as the common foundation, a relic of colonial history that has been adapted and refashioned to suit the needs of modern Nigerian life. It is the language of formality, utilized in corporate boardrooms, government offices, and educational settings. However, the predominance of English doesn't diminish the importance of indigenous languages, especially Yoruba, the dominant mother tongue in Lagos.

In marketplaces, public transport hubs, and among friends and family, Pidgin English often takes center stage. Unlike conventional English, Pidgin is an evolving, adaptive form of communication, a lingua franca that facilitates interaction across diverse ethnic and linguistic backgrounds. Here, the cadence and intonation are different; it's less about grammatical precision and more about mutual understanding. Pidgin is a succinct, direct medium, full of idiomatic expressions and colloquialisms that capture the essence of local life. A sentence like "How you dey?" seamlessly replaces the more formal "How are you?"—a small yet significant shift that demonstrates the informality and accessibility of Pidgin.

Yet, to fully comprehend Lagos's linguistic landscape, one must also appreciate the role of Yoruba. Widely spoken and deeply rooted in tradition, Yoruba not only functions as a means of daily communication but also carries cultural and historical significance. Greeting someone in Yoruba, even with a simple "E kaaro" (Good morning), often garners a warm response and is seen as a gesture of respect and cultural sensitivity. Beyond Yoruba, Lagos remains a confluence of various tribes, and you will often hear Igbo and Hausa spoken among their respective communities, adding to the rich linguistic mosaic of the city.

Learning Pidgin English and Local Slang

For those freshly arrived in Lagos, mastering Pidgin English can be as daunting as it is essential. The first key to learning Pidgin is to embrace its fluid nature. Unlike standard English with its strict grammatical rules, Pidgin is open to interpretation. It is the language of the streets, profoundly democratic and perpetually adaptive. Expressions such as "Wetin dey happen?" (What is happening?) or "I no sabi" (I don't know) might initially sound unfamiliar, but they soon become second nature as you immerse yourself in daily interactions.

However, simply understanding the words isn't enough. One must also grasp the cultural context in which these phrases are used. For instance, the term "Oga" can denote respect and authority, similar to calling someone "boss" or "sir," but its usage is nuanced. Depending on the tone and context, it might convey camaraderie or, conversely, subtle irony. Similarly, "Wahala" means trouble or problems—knowing when to use it can mean the difference between blending in and standing out awkwardly.

Moreover, local slang and colloquialisms can be riddled with metaphors and idioms that may not make immediate sense to an outsider. For example, saying someone has "long throat" refers to greed or an insatiable desire, and to be "janded" means to travel abroad, especially to England—likely derived from the slang term "Naija" for Nigeria. Picking up on these nuances involves more than just rote memorization; it requires active listening and engagement with the people around you.

Communication Challenges and Misunderstandings

Despite the fluidity and adaptability of Pidgin English, communication in Lagos isn't always seamless. Misunderstandings are inevitable, especially for newcomers still tuning their ears to the local vernacular. Early on, it's easy to get lost in translation, misinterpret gestures, or miss the subtext imbued in casual conversations.

One common hurdle is the pace and rhythm of speech. In Lagos, conversations can be rapid-fire, animated exchanges where gestures, tone, and facial expressions play critical roles. The musicality of Yoruba, the staccato briskness of Igbo, and the fluidity of Pidgin all contribute to a rich auditory environment that can overwhelm an unaccustomed listener. An innocuous question might come across as confrontational if the speaker's tonal inflections are misunderstood. Similarly, overlapping conversations, a staple in bustling environments like markets and bus stations, can further complicate comprehension.

Moreover, certain gestures or phrases may carry specific, culturally rooted connotations. Direct eye contact, for instance, might be perceived as assertive or even aggressive, depending on the context. Handshakes and greetings often have their own sets of rules—failing to adhere to them can result in awkward or even offensive interactions. The phrase "I dey come," which means "I am coming," doesn't imply immediate action but rather a flexible, often delayed response.

Overcoming these challenges requires patience, openness, and a sense of humor. It's important to remember that mistakes are part of the learning process. Many Lagosians are understanding and willing to correct missteps, often with a laugh and encouragement. As a newcomer, displaying genuine effort and humility goes a long way in building rapport and easing communication hurdles.

The Role of Language in Social Interactions

Language in Lagos serves as more than just a means of communication; it's a gateway to understanding the city's social fabric. The way people speak, the words they choose, and the languages they use offer insights into social hierarchies, cultural affiliations, and even economic status.

For instance, in professional settings, spoken English often marks formality and preparedness. Meetings, corporate communications, and official documents tend to favor standard English, reflecting the importance placed on education and professionalism. Speaking fluent English in these contexts can be seen as a marker of education and social standing.

Conversely, Pidgin serves as an equalizer in more informal settings, breaking down barriers between diverse ethnic and social groups. It's the preferred mode of communication among friends, in markets, and on the streets. Using Pidgin can foster a sense of camaraderie and belonging, signaling an understanding of and respect for local culture. It allows for a more relaxed, approachable interaction free from the confines of formal English.

Moreover, Yoruba and other indigenous languages often underscore cultural identity and familial bonds. Among Yoruba speakers, using proverbs and idiomatic expressions is a sign of wisdom and cultural literacy. These expressions, rich in metaphors and historical references, encapsulate collective wisdom and social norms, offering a deeper connection to the cultural roots of the community. For instance, the Yoruba proverb "A kii k'ogbon ori like kaakiri" translates to "One does not learn wisdom from experience without traveling far and wide," illustrating the value placed on experience and openness to the world.

Understanding the interplay of these languages and their social implications can significantly enhance one's social interactions in Lagos. Language becomes a tool not just for communicating information but for building relationships, establishing trust, and navigating the complexities of daily life in this vibrant city.

In essence, the linguistic landscape of Lagos is as bustling and dynamic as the city itself. Adapting to this environment requires more than just learning vocabulary and grammar; it demands a willingness to engage with the culture, embrace the nuances, and appreciate the rich tapestry of communication that defines life in Lagos. With time, patience, and openness, newcomers can transform language from a barrier into a bridge, connecting them to the heart and soul of this remarkable megacity.

Chapter 7: Power Struggles: Electricity and Water

As you settle into your life in Lagos, you quickly realize that power and water issues will become part of your daily struggles. The city's infrastructure often struggles to keep up with the of its growing population, resulting in frequent power outages and water scarcity. In this chapter, we will delve into the challenges of dealing with electricity and water in Lagos, exploring the impact these issues have on daily life and the innovative solutions residents have developed to cope with these power struggles.

Coping with frequent power outages

One of the most aspects of living in Lagos is the prevalence of power outages. The city's electricity supply is often unreliable, with frequent blackouts interrupting daily routines. Whether you are at home, at work, or out and about in the city, the sudden loss of power can disrupt your plans and activities. As you navigate life in Lagos, learning to cope with these frequent outages becomes essential.

Residents often rely on generators to provide backup power during outages, but these come with their own challenges. The noise, pollution, and maintenance requirements of generators add to the complexities of dealing with power outages. Understanding how to manage your energy needs, plan for disruptions, and minimize the impact of blackouts on your daily life is a crucial skill for living in Lagos.

Water scarcity and conservation techniques

In addition to power challenges, water scarcity is another significant issue in Lagos. Access to clean, reliable water is not guaranteed for all residents, leading to water shortages and the need to implement conservation techniques.

Whether you live in a high-rise apartment building or a suburban house, managing your water usage and dealing with intermittent supply become part of your routine.

Residents often resort to storing water in tanks or containers to ensure a constant supply during shortages. However, maintaining water quality and hygiene standards can be a concern when relying on stored water. Understanding how to conserve water, reduce wastage, and purify or treat stored water for safety are crucial skills for navigating the water challenges in Lagos.

The generator economy and its impact

Generators play a significant role in the daily lives of Lagos residents, forming the backbone of the city's power supply during outages. The generator economy consists of businesses and individuals that provide generator services, fuel, maintenance, and repairs to keep the city powered during blackouts. Understanding how this informal economy functions and the role it plays in sustaining daily life in Lagos is essential for newcomers.

Despite the challenges and costs associated with generators, they are a lifeline for many households and businesses in Lagos. The reliance on backup power sources highlights the urgent need for improved electricity infrastructure and sustainable solutions to the city's power struggles. Exploring the impact of the generator economy on residents' daily lives and the environment sheds light on the complexities of living in a city where power outages are the norm.

Innovative solutions to utility challenges

Amidst the power struggles and water scarcity in Lagos, residents have developed innovative solutions to address these utility challenges. From solar power systems and rainwater harvesting to community initiatives for water conservation and energy efficiency, there are creative approaches to mitigating the impact of infrastructure deficiencies. Exploring these innovative solutions provides insights into the resilience and adaptability of Lagos residents in the face of utility challenges.

As you navigate the power struggles of electricity and water in Lagos, embracing these innovative solutions and integrating them into your daily life can help you thrive in the face of adversity. By learning from the experiences of long-time residents and adopting sustainable practices, you can make a positive impact on your community and contribute to the collective efforts to address utility challenges in this bustling megacity.

Chapter 8: Social Life in the Megacity

————

Welcome to the vibrant social scene of Lagos, where connections, friendships, and entertainment options abound. In this chapter, we delve into the multifaceted aspects of social life in the bustling megacity. From building relationships with locals and expatriates to exploring the diverse nightlife and entertainment opportunities, Lagos offers a dynamic and enriching social landscape that reflects the city's cultural richness and diversity.

Building Friendships with Locals and Expatriates

One of the most rewarding experiences of living in Lagos is the opportunity to forge meaningful connections with a wide range of people. Whether you're interacting with friendly locals eager to share their culture and traditions or engaging with expatriates who share the experience of navigating life in the megacity, building friendships is a key aspect of social life in Lagos. The city's welcoming atmosphere and vibrant community make it easy to connect with like-minded individuals and expand your social network.

Quote: "Lagos is a melting pot of cultures, and the friendships you cultivate here can be both enriching and enduring. Embrace the diversity and open yourself up to new experiences."

Nightlife and Entertainment Options

Lagos truly comes alive after dark, offering a plethora of

entertainment options for residents and visitors alike. From trendy bars and clubs to live music venues and cultural events, the city's nightlife scene caters to a variety of tastes and preferences. Whether you're looking to dance the night away, enjoy a live performance, or simply relax with friends over drinks, Lagos has something for everyone. The vibrant nightlife reflects the city's energetic spirit and provides a glimpse into its dynamic cultural scene.

Quote: "Experience the infectious energy of Lagos nightlife, where music, laughter, and good company create unforgettable memories. Embrace the rhythm of the city and immerse yourself in its vibrant social scene."

Attending Social Gatherings and Events

Social gatherings and events play a significant role in Lagos's social fabric, offering opportunities to connect with others, celebrate special occasions, and participate in community activities. From birthday parties and weddings to cultural festivals and art exhibitions, Lagos provides a rich tapestry of social events that showcase the city's diversity and creativity. Attending these gatherings allows you to immerse yourself in local traditions, forge new connections, and create lasting memories in this bustling urban environment.

Quote: "Join in the celebrations and festivities that define Lagos's social calendar. From traditional ceremonies to modern events, each gathering offers a unique window into the city's vibrant culture and lively community spirit."

Navigating Cultural Differences in Social Settings

As you navigate the social landscape of Lagos, you may

encounter cultural differences and nuances that shape interpersonal interactions and social dynamics. Understanding and respecting these cultural variations is essential for building authentic relationships and engaging meaningfully with the community. Whether it's learning local customs, observing social norms, or adapting to different communication styles, navigating cultural differences enriches your social experiences and fosters mutual understanding in this diverse megacity.

Quote: "Cultural diversity is the heartbeat of Lagos, where respect for different traditions and beliefs fosters a harmonious social environment. Embrace the city's cultural tapestry and embrace the richness of its social interactions."

Transitioning from the business-oriented aspects of Lagos to its vibrant social scene, Chapter 8 delves into the interpersonal dynamics, entertainment opportunities, and cultural experiences that define the city's social life. Join us in exploring the diverse social landscape of Lagos, where friendships flourish, nightlife thrives, and community connections deepen in this dynamic urban environment.

Chapter 9: The Business of Lagos

As we delve into the tapestry of life in Lagos, it becomes evident that business and entrepreneurship form vital threads in the city's fabric. Lagos, as Nigeria's economic powerhouse, offers a vibrant and dynamic environment for both local and foreign ventures. Chapter 9 navigates through the bustling business landscape, shedding light on the intricacies of the local economy, the spirit of entrepreneurship, networking opportunities, and the myriad challenges and rewards that come with doing business in this megacity.

Understanding the Local Economy

At the heart of Lagos lies a kaleidoscope of economic activities that drive the city's growth and development. From traditional sectors like agriculture, manufacturing, and trade to emerging industries like technology, entertainment, and finance, the city presents a diverse and dynamic economic landscape. Understanding the nuances of the local economy is crucial for anyone looking to establish a business or engage in commercial activities in Lagos.

Local markets and informal economies play a pivotal role in the city's economic ecosystem, providing livelihoods for a significant portion of the population. Learning to navigate these markets, embrace their vibrancy, and leverage their unique opportunities are essential skills for entrepreneurs and business owners in Lagos.

Entrepreneurship and Informal Markets

Entrepreneurship is deeply ingrained in the entrepreneurial spirit of Lagosians, many of whom have turned adversity into opportunities by creating innovative solutions to local challenges. The city's informal markets, characterized by street vendors, roadside businesses, and makeshift stalls, offer a unique glimpse into the resilience and creativity of Lagos residents.

Engaging with the informal economy requires a nuanced understanding of its dynamics, including the role of informal networks, economic survival strategies, and the ethical considerations that accompany such ventures. Entrepreneurs who navigate this terrain with sensitivity and adaptability often find themselves tapping into a rich source of inspiration, collaboration, and resourcefulness.

Networking and Professional Opportunities

In a city as bustling and diverse as Lagos, networking plays a crucial role in establishing business connections, fostering professional relationships, and unlocking new opportunities. From industry conferences and business forums to social events and cultural gatherings, the city offers a myriad of avenues for networking and collaboration.

Building a robust professional network in Lagos requires a blend of authenticity, cultural sensitivity, and strategic vision. Nurturing relationships with local stakeholders, government officials, industry leaders, and fellow entrepreneurs can open doors to new partnerships, investments, and market insights that are crucial for business success in the city.

Challenges and Rewards of Doing Business in Lagos

While Lagos presents a plethora of opportunities for business growth and innovation, it also poses significant challenges that entrepreneurs must navigate with resilience and adaptability. The city's infrastructural deficits, bureaucratic hurdles, regulatory complexities, and security concerns can create obstacles for business operations and expansion.

Overcoming these challenges requires a combination of strategic planning, risk management, and proactive engagement with local authorities and stakeholders. Entrepreneurs who successfully navigate the intricate web of challenges in Lagos often find themselves reaping the rewards of a vibrant market, a diverse talent pool, and a resilient consumer base that is receptive to new ideas and innovative solutions.

In conclusion, Chapter 9 provides a comprehensive overview of the business landscape in Lagos, offering insights into the local economy, entrepreneurship opportunities, networking strategies, and the challenges and rewards of doing business in one of Africa's most dynamic cities. By embracing the spirit of innovation, collaboration, and perseverance, entrepreneurs can unlock the vast potential that Lagos has to offer, contributing to the city's economic growth and societal development.

Chapter 10: Faith and Spirituality

As we delve into the fabric of, it becomes evident that one cannot ignore the profound influence of faith and spirituality that permeates the city. Lagos, a melting pot of cultures and religions, offers rich tapestry of beliefs shape the daily lives and interactions of its diverse inhabitants. In this chapter, we explore the intricate interplay of religious diversity, the impact of faith on culture, experiences with local churches and mosques, and the spiritual practices and superstitions that form an integral part Lagos life.

Religious Diversity in LagosLagos stands as a shining example of religious pluralism, where Christianity, Islam, traditional African religions, and various other faith systems coexist harmoniously. The city boasts an array of churches, mosques, temples, and shrines that cater to the spiritual needs of its multi-faith population. From the grand cathedrals of the Christian denominations to the majestic minarets of the Islamic faith, Lagos showcases a colorful mosaic of worship spaces that reflect the religious diversity of its people.

The presence of vibrant religious communities contributes to the social cohesion and cultural vibrancy of Lagos, fostering an environment where individuals from different backgrounds can come together in a spirit of mutual respect and understanding. The peaceful coexistence of various faith traditions in the city serves as a testament to the inclusive and tolerant nature of its residents.

Impact of Faith on Daily Life and Culture

Faith serves as a guiding force in the lives of many Lagosians, influencing their daily decisions, ethical conduct, and social interactions. Whether it be through prayers offered at dawn in mosques or the joyful hymns sung in Sunday church services, religion plays a central role in shaping the moral compass and worldview of individuals across the city.

The values and teachings espoused by different religious traditions permeate various aspects of Lagosian culture, influencing art, music, literature, and community life. From the celebration of religious holidays to the observance of spiritual rituals and ceremonies, faith weaves a common thread that binds the fabric of Lagos society together, fostering a sense of shared identity and collective belonging.

Experiences with Local Churches and Mosques

Lagos boasts a plethora of vibrant religious congregations that cater to the spiritual needs of its residents. From the charismatic megachurches that attract thousands of worshippers to the serene mosques that echo with the sound of adhan, the city offers a diverse array of places of worship where individuals can commune with the divine.

For many Lagosians, the church or mosque serves not only as a spiritual sanctuary but also as a social hub where they form bonds of friendship, seek guidance from religious leaders, and engage in acts of charitable service. The communal aspect of religious life in Lagos fosters a sense of camaraderie and solidarity among believers, creating tight-knit communities that offer support and companionship in times of joy and adversity.

Spiritual Practices and Superstitions

In addition to organized religion, Lagos is home to a rich tapestry of spiritual practices and superstitions that reflect the syncretic nature of its cultural landscape. From traditional healing ceremonies to the veneration of spiritual deities and ancestral spirits, the city teems with a diverse array of belief systems that blend indigenous traditions with external influences.

Superstitions and folk beliefs also play a prominent role in the lives of many Lagosians, shaping their perceptions of luck, fate, and fortune. Practices such as wearing protective amulets, consulting diviners for guidance, and observing taboos and rituals underscore the deep-rooted supernatural beliefs that underpin daily life in the city, adding a layer of mystique and intrigue to the urban experience.

In exploring the intricate tapestry of faith and spirituality that defines Lagos, one gains a deeper appreciation for the cultural richness and diversity that characterize this dynamic megacity. From the grandiose places of worship to the intimate rituals of daily devotion, religion serves as a cornerstone of identity and community in the lives of its inhabitants, offering solace, inspiration, and a sense of belonging in the bustling urban landscape.

Chapter 11: Fashion and Style in Lagos

As we delve into the vibrant and dynamic city of Lagos, Nigeria, there is an undeniable aspect that colors the daily interactions and aesthetics of its residents - the fashion and style that permeate every corner of this bustling metropolis. In this chapter, we will explore the richstry of traditional and modern fashion trends that define Lagos society, the significance of appearance in social circles, the experience of shopping for clothes and accessories, and the nuances of adapting personal style to local norms.

Traditional and Modern Fashion Trends

Lagos is a city where tradition seamlessly intertwines with modernity, and this cultural fusion is most evident in the fashion choices of its people. Traditional Nigerian attire such as the elegant Yoruba "iro and buba" or the colorful Igbo "isi agu" are proudly displayed during cultural events and special occasions. These outfits, adorned with intricate embroidery and vibrant patterns, symbolize heritage and identity.

Conversely, Lagosians also embrace contemporary fashion trends from around the globe. The streets of Lagos are fashion runways, showcasing bold colors, avant-garde designs, and a mix of high-end luxury brands and local designers. From casual streetwear to red-carpet glamour, the fashion scene in Lagos is a melting pot of creativity and expression, reflecting the city's cosmopolitan flair.

The Importance of Appearance in Lagos Society

In Lagos, appearance is not merely about looking good; it is a form of communication, a language spoken without words. The way you dress in Lagos conveys messages about your social status, personality, and even your aspirations. As such, there is immense pressure to present oneself well in various settings, whether at work, social gatherings, or religious ceremonies.

The emphasis on appearance extends beyond clothing to grooming, accessories, and overall presentation. Lagosians take pride in their appearance, investing time and resources into maintaining a polished look. The "Lagos look" is sleek, sophisticated, and always on-trend, showcasing a blend of elegance and confidence that is synonymous with the city's fashion-forward culture.

Shopping for Clothes and Accessories

Navigating the labyrinth of fashion boutiques, markets, and shopping malls in Lagos can be both exhilarating and overwhelming. From the upscale boutiques of Victoria Island to the bustling markets of Balogun and Yaba, Lagos offers a diverse shopping experience for every budget and style preference. Trendy boutiques showcase the latest designer collections, while traditional markets brim with handcrafted fabrics, beaded jewelry, and unique accessories.

The art of bargaining is a crucial skill when shopping in Lagos, as haggling is not only expected but celebrated. The negotiation process is a social dance between buyer and seller, where prices are debated, discounts are offered, and relationships are forged through the shared experience of commerce. Building rapport with local vendors can lead to insider deals and access to exclusive pieces, fostering a sense of community within the fashion marketplace.

Adapting Personal Style to Local Norms

For expatriates and newcomers to Lagos, navigating the unspoken rules of fashion and style in the city can be a rewarding yet challenging experience. Understanding the cultural nuances of dress codes, acceptable attire for different occasions, and the importance of modesty in certain settings are essential aspects of acclimating to Lagosian society. By observing and emulating local fashion trends, residents can integrate seamlessly into the fabric of Lagos life, forging connections and expressing respect for the city's cultural heritage.

In conclusion, fashion and style in Lagos are not just about clothing; they are a reflection of identity, status, and cultural heritage. By embracing the city's sartorial diversity, residents can participate in a visual dialogue that celebrates tradition, innovation, and individual expression. As we navigate the bustling streets and vibrant markets of Lagos, we are reminded that fashion is not just a statement; it is a story waiting to be told.

Chapter 12: Health and Wellness Challenges

<hr>

Health is a fundamental aspect of life that impacts our overall well-being, productivity, and happiness. Living in a bustling megacity like Lagos presents unique health and wellness challenges due to various factors such as healthcare accessibility, tropical diseases, environmental issues, and stressors associated with urban living. In this chapter, we will explore the intricacies navigating the healthcare system, managing tropical diseases, finding balance in a hectic city environment, and addressing mental health concerns in Lagos### Navigating the Healthcare System

Accessing quality healthcare is a primary concern for residents of Lagos, given the city's burgeoning population and limited healthcare infrastructure. The healthcare system in Lagos comprises a mix of public and private hospitals, clinics, and healthcare providers, each offering varying levels of care and services. Navigating this complex healthcare landscape requires an understanding of available healthcare facilities, insurance coverage, and medical specialties.

Public hospitals in Lagos, such as the Lagos University Teaching Hospital (LUTH) and the General Hospital, provide essential healthcare services to a significant portion of the population. However, these facilities often face challenges such as overcrowding, long wait times, and resource constraints. Private hospitals and clinics offer an alternative for those seeking more personalized and efficient care, albeit at a higher cost. Navigating the healthcare system involves choosing healthcare providers based on reputation, recommendations, and your specific healthcare needs.

Dealing with Tropical Diseases and Health Risks

Lagos, like many tropical regions, is prone to a range of infectious diseases and health risks that can pose significant challenges to residents' health. Malaria, typhoid fever, cholera, and yellow fever are prevalent in Lagos, requiring proactive measures such as vaccinations, mosquito control, and safe food and water practices to mitigate the risk of contracting these diseases.

Malaria, transmitted by mosquitoes, remains a major health concern in Lagos and accounts for a significant portion of healthcare visits. Taking anti-malarial medication, using mosquito nets, and avoiding mosquito bites are essential preventive measures. Typhoid fever, a bacterial infection spread through contaminated food and water, is another common health risk in Lagos, emphasizing the importance of maintaining proper hygiene and safe food practices.

Additionally, waterborne diseases like cholera and gastrointestinal infections are prevalent in Lagos due to inadequate sanitation and poor water quality. Practicing good hygiene, using clean water sources, and avoiding contaminated food are crucial steps in preventing such diseases. Staying informed about disease outbreaks, seeking timely medical attention, and adhering to preventive healthcare measures are vital in managing health risks in Lagos.

Finding Balance and Maintaining Fitness

The fast-paced lifestyle and demanding work environments

in Lagos can take a toll on one's physical and mental well-being. Finding balance amidst the chaos of urban living is essential for maintaining optimal health and fitness. Incorporating regular exercise, healthy eating habits, and adequate rest into your daily routine can help combat the stresses of city life and promote overall wellness.

Lagos offers various fitness centers, gyms, parks, and recreational facilities where residents can engage in physical activities such as jogging, yoga, swimming, and group fitness classes. Establishing a workout routine that fits your schedule and preferences is key to staying active and healthy. Embracing a balanced diet rich in fruits, vegetables, whole grains, and lean proteins can fuel your body and boost your energy levels, contributing to overall well-being.

Moreover, prioritizing mental health is crucial in managing stress and maintaining emotional equilibrium in a bustling city like Lagos. Engaging in relaxation techniques, mindfulness practices, and seeking professional help when needed can support mental health resilience and coping mechanisms. Creating a supportive social network, practicing self-care, and setting boundaries to protect your well-being are integral aspects of finding balance and maintaining optimal health in Lagos.

Transition to Chapter 13: Arts and Culture Scene

Exploring the vibrant arts and cultural landscape of Lagos offers a multifaceted glimpse into the city's rich heritage, creative expressions, and cultural dynamism. From museums and galleries to Nollywood films and music performances, Lagos' arts scene reflects the

diversity, creativity, and artistic prowess that define this megacity. In the upcoming chapter, we will delve into the nexus of arts, culture, and creativity in Lagos, uncovering the myriad forms of artistic expression that shape the city's identity and soul.

Chapter 13: Arts and Culture Scene

As we delve into the vibrant arts and landscape of Lagos, we are met with a tapestry of creativity, tradition, and innovation that defines the city's unique identity. From museums showcasing rich heritage to the bustling industry of Nollywood, from the rhythmic beats of Afrobeat music to contemporary art exhibitions and cultural festivals, Lagos offers a diverse array of artistic experiences that captivate residents and visitors alike. This chapter explores the multifaceted world of arts and culture in the megacity, shedding light on the dynamic expressions that shape its social fabric.

Exploring Museums and Galleries

Lagos boasts a rich history that is preserved and celebrated in various museums and galleries scattered throughout the city. From the iconic National Museum in Onikan to the Nike Art Gallery in Lekki, these cultural institutions offer a glimpse into the past, present, and future of Nigeria's artistic heritage. Visitors can immerse themselves in traditional artifacts, indigenous crafts, and contemporary artworks that reflect the country's diverse cultural heritage. The museum experience in Lagos is not just about viewing exhibits but engaging with the stories, struggles, and triumphs of a nation through its art.

Nollywood and the Film Industry

No exploration of Lagos's cultural scene would be complete without mentioning Nollywood, the thriving Nigerian film industry that has garnered global recognition for its prolific output and unique storytelling. Nollywood, often referred to as the "third-largest film industry in the world," churns out hundreds of movies annually, ranging from melodramatic blockbusters to thought-provoking independent films. The accessibility and grassroots nature of Nollywood have made it a cultural phenomenon, shaping entertainment preferences and amplifying Nigerian voices on the global stage. The chapter of Lagos's film industry is a testament to the city's creative spirit and storytelling prowess.

Music and Live Performances

Music pulses through the veins of Lagos, resonating in every corner of the city from roadside bars to concert halls. The sounds of Afrobeat, highlife, juju, and contemporary genres blend harmoniously, reflecting the diverse musical influences that permeate Nigerian culture. Live performances are a staple of Lagos's nightlife, where local artists and international acts converge to create unforgettable experiences for music enthusiasts. Whether it's an intimate jazz session at a cozy lounge or a lively Afrobeat concert under the stars, Lagos offers a kaleidoscope of sonic delights that cater to every taste and mood.

Contemporary Art and Cultural Festivals

Lagos's contemporary art scene is a dynamic playground where experimentation, expression, and activism collide to redefine artistic boundaries. Galleries like Art Twenty One, Omenka Gallery, and Rele Gallery showcase the works of emerging and established artists who challenge conventional norms and provoke thought through their creations. The city's cultural festivals, such as the Lagos Theatre Festival, Lagos Fashion Week, and Lagos International Poetry Festival, bring together creatives from various disciplines to celebrate diversity, inclusion, and artistic excellence. These platforms serve as catalysts for cultural dialogue, intercultural exchange, and community engagement, fostering a vibrant ecosystem for artists and audiences to connect and collaborate.

In conclusion, Lagos's arts and culture scene is a dynamic tapestry of creativity, tradition, and innovation that reflects the city's rich heritage and contemporary spirit. From museums and galleries that preserve Nigeria's diverse cultural legacy to the bustling film industry of Nollywood and the pulsating beats of Afrobeat music, Lagos offers a myriad of artistic experiences that resonate with residents and visitors alike. Through exploration, engagement, and appreciation of the arts, we gain a deeper understanding of the city's soul and contribute to the vibrant tapestry of cultural expression that defines Lagos as a creative hub in Africa.

Chapter 14: Education and Learning

Education plays a pivotal role in shaping society, and Lagos is no exception. In this chapter, we delve into the local education system, opportunities for adult learning, cultural exchange programs, and the significance education in the vibrant city of Lagos.

Insights into the Local Education System

Lagos boasts a diverse educational landscape, catering to children and adults alike. From primary schools to universities, the city offers a array of educational institutions Public schools provide education to a significant of the population, while private schools offer specialized curricula and facilities. Understanding the nuances of the local education system is crucial for residents and newcomers alike.

Adult Learning and Skill Development Opportunities

Learning doesn't stop after formal education ends. Lagos provides various opportunities for adults to acquire new skills, pursue further education, and engage in lifelong learning. Vocational training centers, workshops, and online courses cater to individuals looking to enhance their professional capabilities or explore new interests.

Cultural Exchange and Mutual Learning Experiences

Lagos serves as a melting pot of cultures, offering

unparalleled opportunities for cultural exchange and mutual learning. Interactions between locals and expatriates create a dynamic environment where ideas, traditions, and perspectives converge. Engaging with different cultures broadens horizons and fosters mutual understanding among diverse communities.

The Value of Education in Lagos Society

Education holds immense value in Lagos society, shaping economic opportunities, social mobility, and personal development. Families prioritize education for their children, viewing it as a pathway to success and empowerment. Educated individuals often contribute positively to the community, driving innovation, progress, and social change.

Education in Lagos is not merely about academic achievement; it is a transformative experience that transcends borders and cultural barriers. Embracing the educational opportunities available in the city can lead to personal growth, career advancement, and a deeper understanding of the world around us.

With a commitment to learning and an openness to new experiences, residents of Lagos can harness the power of education to shape a brighter future for themselves and their communities. As we navigate the complexities of the local education landscape, let us appreciate the transformative impact of learning in this bustling megacity.

Chapter 15: Environmental Realities

———

Lagos, Nigeria's bustling megacity, faces a myriad of environmental challenges that significantly impact the daily lives of its residents. From pollution and waste management issues to climate change impacts, the city is at the forefront of dealing with pressing environmental concerns. This chapter delves deep into the environmental realities of Lagos, exploring the various issues at play and the innovative solutions being implemented to address them.

Pollution and Waste Management Issues

LAGOS, LIKE MANY RAPIDLY growing urban centers, grapples with high levels of pollution across various fronts. Air pollution from vehicular exhaust, industrial activities, and open waste burning poses serious health risks to the city's inhabitants. The visible smog that blankets the city during rush hours is a stark reminder of the air quality challenges faced by Lagosians.

Moreover, waste management remains a significant challenge in Lagos. With a population exceeding 20 million people, the city generates massive amounts of waste daily. Inadequate infrastructure for waste collection and disposal has led to widespread littering, illegal dumpsites, and uncontrolled waste burning, further contributing to environmental degradation. The chapter explores the root causes of these issues and highlights community-driven initiatives aimed at cleaning up the city.

Climate Change Impacts on the City

THE EFFECTS OF CLIMATE change are being felt in Lagos, from unpredictable weather patterns to rising sea levels that threaten coastal communities. The city's low-lying geography makes it particularly vulnerable to flooding, a problem exacerbated by poor drainage systems and inadequate urban planning. Each year, the rainy season brings with it the risk of devastating floods that displace thousands of residents and disrupt economic activities.

Furthermore, the urban heat island effect is noticeable in Lagos, as rapid urbanization leads to the replacement of green spaces with concrete structures. This phenomenon results in higher ambient temperatures, affecting the health and well-being of residents.

The chapter discusses ongoing climate adaptation efforts in Lagos, such as resilient infrastructure projects and green space conservation initiatives.

Grassroots Environmental Initiatives

AMIDST THE ENVIRONMENTAL challenges facing Lagos, there is a growing movement of grassroots initiatives aimed at promoting sustainable practices and raising awareness about environmental issues. Community-based organizations, NGOs, and concerned citizens are coming together to tackle pollution, waste management, and climate change mitigation in innovative ways.

One such initiative is the "Clean Lagos" campaign, which mobilizes volunteers for regular clean-up exercises in neighborhoods across the city. These efforts not only improve the aesthetic appeal of Lagos but also foster a sense of environmental consciousness among its residents. Additionally, tree planting programs, recycling projects, and educational workshops are empowering communities to take ownership of their environment and drive positive change.

Adapting to Environmental Challenges

AS LAGOS GRAPPLES WITH its environmental realities, there is a growing recognition of the interconnectedness between human activities and ecosystem health. Sustainable urban planning, green technologies, and public awareness campaigns are crucial components of the city's efforts to adapt to environmental challenges. By promoting eco-friendly practices, reducing carbon emissions, and conserving natural resources, Lagos is striving to create a healthier and more sustainable future for its residents.

In conclusion, the environmental realities of Lagos underscore the urgent need for collective action to protect the city's natural environment and ensure the well-being of its inhabitants. By embracing innovative solutions, raising awareness, and fostering a culture of environmental stewardship, Lagos can pave the way for a greener, cleaner, and more resilient urban landscape.

Chapter 16: Technology and Innovation

Lagos, Nigeria's bustling megacity, has transformed significantly in recent years, embracing technology and innovation to navigate daily challenges and drive economic growth. From the rise tech startups to the increased connectivity of its citizens, Lagos is at the forefront of technological advancement in Africa. This chapter delves into the role of technology in shaping the city's, exploring how it daily life, business opportunities, and cultural experiences.

The Role of Technology in Daily Lagos Life

TECHNOLOGY PERMEATES every aspect of daily in Lagos, from communication to transportation. With the widespread adoption of smartphones and the internet, Lagosians are increasingly connected to the digital world. Mobile applications have revolutionized the way people navigate the city, enabling them to order rides, food deliveries, and even groceries with a few taps on their smartphones. The convenience offered by these tech-driven solutions has significantly improved the quality of life for Lagos residents, making it easier to access essential services and products.

Internet Connectivity and Digital Culture

ONE OF THE MOST SIGNIFICANT technological advancements in Lagos has been the expansion of internet connectivity. With the proliferation of affordable smartphones and data plans, more Lagosians have access to the internet than ever before. This increased connectivity has fueled a burgeoning digital culture in the city, with social media platforms becoming vital tools for communication, networking, and business promotion. Lagosians are active users of platforms like Twitter, Facebook, and Instagram, using these channels to share information, express opinions, and connect with others.

Tech Startups and Innovation Hubs

LAGOS HAS EMERGED AS a hub for tech startups and innovation, attracting entrepreneurs and investors from around the world. The city's vibrant ecosystem of incubators, accelerators, and co-working spaces has nurtured a generation of visionary founders, driving innovation in diverse sectors such as fintech, e-commerce, health tech, and agritech. These startups are not only creating jobs and wealth but also addressing pressing social issues, such as access to financial services, healthcare delivery, and agricultural productivity. Lagos is home to groundbreaking startups like Paystack, Flutterwave, Andela, and many others, making significant contributions to Nigeria's growing digital economy.

Balancing Tradition and Technological Advancement

WHILE TECHNOLOGY HAS brought about immense benefits to Lagos, it also poses challenges in balancing tradition with modernity. As the city rapidly urbanizes and digitizes, there is a need to preserve cultural heritage and traditional practices. Lagosians are navigating this balance by incorporating technology into their daily routines while upholding customs and values that define their identity. From celebrating traditional festivals to promoting local crafts, Lagosians are finding innovative ways to merge tradition with innovation, creating a unique cultural tapestry that sets the city apart.

Conclusion and Transition

AS LAGOS CONTINUES to evolve as a tech-savvy metropolis, the integration of technology into various facets of life is reshaping the city's future. From improving efficiency and convenience to fostering entrepreneurship and creativity, technology plays a pivotal role in driving progress and innovation in Lagos. The next chapter will explore the dynamics of family life and relationships in the megacity, shedding light on the intricacies of social interactions and domestic arrangements in this vibrant urban environment.

Chapter 17: Family Life and Relationships

———

L ife in Lagos is not just about the work environment or exploring the vibrant cultural scene. It also involves understanding the intricate dynamics of family life and relationships in this bustling megacity. From observing family structures to managing romantic connections, this chapter delves into the multifaceted aspects of personal relationships that shape the social fabric of Lagos.

Observing Family Dynamics in Lagos

LAGOS IS A CITY WHERE family ties run deep, and the concept of family beyond the nuclear unit. Extended families often live in close proximity providing a strong support system for individuals. It is common to see generations residing under one roof, sharing responsibilities and building bonds that transcend time and distance. Observing these intricate family dynamics offers a glimpse into the rich tapestry of Lagosian life.

Families in Lagos place a high value on traditions and customs, which are passed down from generation to generation. From celebratory rituals to daily routines, these traditions form the very foundation of family life in the city. Understanding and respecting these customs are essential for integrating into the social fabric of Lagos and forging meaningful relationships with local communities.

Dating and Romance in the City

NAVIGATING THE DATING scene in Lagos requires a delicate balance of tradition and modernity. While some individuals still adhere to traditional courtship practices, many embrace contemporary dating norms influenced by Western culture and urban lifestyles. Meeting potential partners often occurs through social gatherings, work settings, or online platforms, reflecting the diverse pathways to romance in the city.

Romantic relationships in Lagos are shaped by a myriad of factors, including cultural expectations, religious beliefs, and societal norms. Balancing personal desires with external influences can be challenging, especially when navigating the complexities of dating across diverse backgrounds and communities. Approaching relationships with an open mind and respect for differences is key to fostering meaningful connections in the city.

Childcare and Raising Children

FAMILY LIFE IN LAGOS revolves around the well-being and upbringing of children, who are cherished as the future of the community. Childcare practices vary widely, influenced by cultural traditions, economic circumstances, and social expectations. From extended family members pitching in to professional childcare services, parents employ diverse strategies to provide a nurturing environment for their children.

Raising children in Lagos comes with its own set of challenges and rewards. Providing quality education, ensuring healthcare access, and instilling moral values are among the top priorities for families in the city. Navigating the complexities of modern parenting while preserving cultural heritage poses a constant juggling act for many Lagosian families, underscoring the importance of adaptability and resilience in the face of evolving social dynamics.

Maintaining Long-Distance Relationships

IN A CITY AS DYNAMIC as Lagos, maintaining long-distance relationships is a common phenomenon. Whether due to work commitments, educational pursuits, or family obligations, individuals often find themselves navigating the complexities of staying connected across geographical distances. Long-distance relationships require strong communication skills, trust, and mutual respect to thrive amidst the challenges of physical separation.

Technology plays a crucial role in bridging the gap for individuals in long-distance relationships. From video calls to instant messaging, digital platforms provide a lifeline for couples separated by miles, enabling them to share moments, support each other, and foster emotional intimacy despite the physical distance. Balancing the demands of daily life in Lagos with the emotional needs of a long-distance relationship requires patience, understanding, and a commitment to shared goals.

Navigating family life and relationships in Lagos is a nuanced journey that involves embracing tradition while navigating the complexities of contemporary urban living. From observing the rich tapestry of family dynamics to managing romantic connections and childcare responsibilities, individuals in Lagos must adapt to changing social landscapes while cherishing the timeless values that bind families together. In the intricate web of relationships that define life in Lagos, the threads of love, respect, and resilience weave a narrative of connection that transcends

Chapter 18: The Informal Economy

U pon immersing yourself in the vibrant essence of Lagos, one cannot help but be entranced by the myriad informal economic activities that animate the city. The informal economy in Lagos, much like in other African urban centers, plays a significant role in providing livelihoods, fostering entrepreneurship, and meeting the daily needs of its residents. In this chapter, we delve into the intricate web of street vendors, roadside businesses, and informal networks that underpin the socio-economic fabric of Lagos.

Street Vendors and Roadside Businesses

WALKING DOWN THE FRENETIC streets of Lagos, one encounters a kaleidoscope of street vendors peddling their wares, from fresh fruits and snacks to mobile phone accessories and household essentials. These micro-entrepreneurs form the backbone of the informal economy, operating with agility and resilience in the face of regulatory challenges and limited resources. A common sight in Lagos, these vendors offer convenience and affordability to residents while creating a dynamic marketplace that pulsates with energy.

Roadside businesses, ranging from makeshift food stalls to mobile repair workshops, dot the urban landscape, embodying the spirit of ingenuity and resourcefulness that characterizes Lagosians. These enterprises, though often informal in nature, cater to a diverse clientele and contribute to the local economy by providing goods and services in innovative ways. Despite facing constant threats of eviction and regulatory constraints, these businesses persist, adapting to changing circumstances and carving out niches in the bustling cityscape.

The Role of Informal Networks in Daily Life

IN LAGOS, INFORMAL networks play a crucial role in facilitating transactions, disseminating information, and fostering social cohesion. These networks, often based on kinship ties, shared experiences, or common interests, form the social capital that sustains communities and enables individuals to navigate the complexities of urban life. From savings groups that pool resources to support small businesses to community associations that advocate for shared interests, these informal networks embody the spirit of solidarity and mutual assistance that permeates Lagosian society.

Moreover, the informal economy in Lagos thrives on networks of trust and reciprocity, where reputation and relationships drive economic transactions and social interactions. Whether through word-of-mouth referrals, informal credit arrangements, or cooperative ventures, these networks create a sense of belonging and interconnectedness that transcends formal market structures. In the absence of robust institutional support, Lagosians rely on these informal networks to access opportunities, mitigate risks, and foster resilience in the face of adversity.

Economic Survival Strategies of Lagos Residents

FOR MANY LAGOS RESIDENTS, engagement in the informal economy is not just a matter of choice but a necessity dictated by economic constraints and limited formal employment opportunities. As such, individuals develop a myriad of survival strategies to navigate the uncertainties of the informal sector, from diversifying income sources to leveraging social networks for support. Flexibility, adaptability, and creativity are key skills honed by informal entrepreneurs, enabling them to seize opportunities, overcome challenges, and sustain their livelihoods in a competitive urban environment.

Furthermore, informal businesses in Lagos often operate within a complex web of regulations, informal taxes, and market dynamics that demand astute negotiation skills and strategic decision-making. Balancing the need for profitability with ethical considerations, these entrepreneurs navigate ethical dilemmas, social responsibilities, and economic imperatives to sustain their businesses while upholding their values. The informal economy in Lagos is thus a microcosm of the broader socio-economic landscape, reflecting the interplay of individual agency, structural constraints, and cultural norms that shape urban life.

As you explore the vibrant tapestry of the informal economy in Lagos, you will gain insights into the resilience, innovation, and community spirit that define the entrepreneurial spirit of the city. From the bustling markets to the bustling streets, Lagos pulsates with the vitality of informal economic activities that underpin its dynamic urban ecosystem. Embrace the ingenuity, perseverance, and resourcefulness of Lagosians as they navigate the informal economy with flair and finesse, creating opportunities, forging connections, and shaping the future of Africa's largest megacity.

Chapter 19: Lagos After Dark

As the sun sets over the bustling metropolis of Lagos, the megacity transforms into a different entity, pulsating with energy, vibrancy, and a unique charm that comes alive after dark. Chapter 19 delves into the nocturnal world of Lagos, exploring the myriad activities, sights, and sounds that define the city's nightlife and after-hours scene. From safety concerns to 24-hour markets, this chapter provides an in-depth look at what it's like to experience Lagos after dark.

Nighttime Exploration

EXPLORING LAGOS AFTER dark unveils a different side of the city that is often shrouded in mystery during the daytime. The cacophony of daytime traffic is replaced by the rhythmic sounds of music, laughter, and chatter as Lagosians unwind and embrace the night. Neighborhoods come alive with neon lights, street performers, and late-night eateries serving up delectable snacks. From the upscale nightlife districts to the more laid-back local hangouts, Lagos offers a diverse range of options for those looking to explore the city after sunset.

One can venture into the quiet alleyways of Victoria Island, where hidden bars and speakeasies offer a glimpse into Lagos's burgeoning cocktail culture. Alternatively, head to the vibrant streets of Surulere or Ikeja, where live music venues and nightclubs keep the city alive until the early hours. Navigating Lagos after dark requires a keen sense of awareness and an openness to new experiences, making it an exciting adventure for both locals and expatriates alike.

Safety Concerns and Precautions

WHILE LAGOS COMES ALIVE with activity after dark, it's important to exercise caution and be mindful of safety concerns that may arise during nighttime exploration. Like any other major city, Lagos has its fair share of security challenges, especially after dark. From petty crime to more serious incidents, being vigilant and aware of your surroundings is crucial when navigating the city's nightlife.

Traveling in groups, using trusted transportation services, and avoiding poorly lit areas are just some of the precautions that can help mitigate potential risks. Engaging with locals and seeking advice from residents can offer invaluable insights into safe places to visit and areas to avoid. By being proactive and taking necessary safety measures, visitors and residents alike can enjoy all that Lagos after dark has to offer while minimizing potential risks.

24-Hour Markets and Services

A UNIQUE ASPECT OF Lagos after dark is the presence of 24-hour markets and services that cater to the city's round-the-clock lifestyle. Amidst the backdrop of bustling streets and flickering streetlights, one can find an array of markets that remain open well into the night, offering everything from fresh produce to household goods.

The famous Balogun Market in Lagos Island is a prime example of a bustling marketplace that thrives long after sunset, with vendors setting up stalls well into the night to cater to late-night shoppers. The market's vibrant atmosphere, filled with the rich aromas of spices and the calls of enthusiastic sellers, provides a sensory experience unlike any other. Additionally, essential services such as pharmacies, convenience stores, and eateries operate round the clock, ensuring that residents have access to necessities at any hour.

For those looking to experience the pulse of Lagos after dark, exploring these 24-hour markets and services offers a glimpse into the city's resilient spirit and unwavering energy, showcasing how Lagosians adapt to the challenges of urban life and maintain a vibrant economy throughout the night.

In the heart of Lagos, a city that never sleeps, the after-dark allure beckons residents and visitors alike to immerse themselves in the vibrant nightlife and unique experiences that define Lagos after dark. From safety precautions to lively markets, Chapter 19 provides a comprehensive guide to navigating the nocturnal landscape of this dynamic megacity, offering insights into the diverse facets of Lagos's nightlife and the captivating charm that emerges under the cover of night.

Chapter 20: Reflections on a Year in Lagos

Living in Lagos for a year is a transformative experience that leaves an indelible mark on anyone who ventures into this vibrant megacity. It's a city that challenges, surprises, and ultimately changes those who call it home. In this final chapter, we reflect on the journey, the growth, the lessons learned, and the lasting impressions of a year spent navigating life in Lagos, Nigeria.

Personal Growth and Transformation

THE FIRST YEAR IN LAGOS is a whirlwind of experiences that push residents out of their comfort zones and into a world of constant motion and change. From grappling with the chaos of traffic to haggling in markets, each encounter teaches valuable lessons about resilience, adaptability, and patience. Every challenge overcame, every obstacle navigated, contributes to personal growth, fostering a deeper understanding of oneself and the world around.

Embracing the unexpected becomes a way of life, as Lagos demands flexibility and an open mind. The diverse encounters and interactions in this dynamic city broaden perspectives, shatter preconceived notions, and encourage personal evolution. Adapting to the pace, the energy, and the spirit of Lagos unlocks hidden potentials and reveals inner strengths that might have remained dormant in a different environment.

Lessons Learned and Skills Acquired

ONE CANNOT LIVE IN Lagos for a year without picking up a multitude of practical skills and life lessons along the way. From the art of bargaining in crowded markets to navigating the bewildering array of transportation options, each experience adds a new layer of knowledge and capability. Learning to navigate electricity outages and water shortages, finding creative solutions to everyday problems, and adapting to the ever-changing landscape of Lagos equips residents with a resourcefulness that proves invaluable.

Cultural competencies grow as residents immerse themselves in the rich tapestry of Lagos life. Communication skills sharpen as they navigate the city's linguistic landscape, picking up pidgin English and local slang. Interpersonal skills develop as they build relationships across diverse communities, bridging cultural divides and forming connections that transcend borders. Patience, resilience, and adaptability are honed in the crucible of Lagos, preparing residents for any challenge that lies ahead.

Changed Perceptions of Lagos and Nigeria

ARRIVING IN LAGOS WITH a set of preconceptions and stereotypes, residents quickly find that the city defies easy categorization. Lagos is a place of paradoxes, where intense beauty coexists with profound hardship, where vibrant energy mingles with deep-seated challenges. Living in Lagos for a year reshapes perceptions, challenging assumptions and revealing the heart and soul of a city that is constantly in flux.

The stereotypes fall away as residents come to understand the complexity and nuance of Lagos life. The initial shock of the chaos gives way to an appreciation of the city's dynamic spirit, its resilience, and its unwavering optimism. Lagos becomes more than just a physical location; it becomes a state of mind, a way of being that leaves an indelible mark on all who experience it.

Future Outlook and Lasting Impressions

AS THE YEAR IN LAGOS draws to a close, residents are left with a profound sense of gratitude for the experiences, the lessons, and the connections forged in this megacity. Looking towards the future, they carry with them a newfound appreciation for the challenges that enrich and enliven life in Lagos. The city becomes a part of them, influencing their outlook, their decisions, and their aspirations in ways they never imagined.

The lasting impressions of a year in Lagos are as diverse as the city itself. From the vibrant markets to the rich tapestry of cultures, from the hustle of entrepreneurship to the tranquility of the beaches, Lagos leaves an indelible mark on all who dare to embrace its complexities. The year might be over, but the memories, the lessons, and the transformations endure, shaping lives and perspectives far beyond the boundaries of this bustling metropolis.

Book Conclusion

Living in Lagos, Nigeria's bustling megacity, is an experience like no other. It's a city that challenges you, surprises you, and ultimately changes you in ways you never could have imagined. From the chaos of arrival at Murtala Muhammed International Airport to finding a home in the midst of urban sprawl, navigating the maze of transportation, bargaining in vibrant markets, and savoring the flavors of local cuisine, every aspect of life in Lagos is a lesson in resilience and adaptation. It's a place where linguistic diversity, religious harmony, and cultural richness converge to create a unique tapestry of experiences.

As you reflect on your year in Lagos, you realize that the city has shaped you in profound ways. You have learned the art of patience in traffic jams, the skill of negotiation in marketplaces, and the joy of embracing a new language and culture. The challenges of power outages, water scarcity, and healthcare concerns have taught you to appreciate the small victories and find innovative solutions. Your interactions with locals and expatriates have broadened your perspective and deepened your understanding of community and friendship.

In the end, Lagos is not just a city – it's a living, breathing entity that leaves an indelible mark on all who pass through its vibrant streets. Whether you leave with a sense of nostalgia or relief, you carry with you the lessons of resilience, adaptability, and appreciation for the beauty that can be found even in the chaos. As you bid farewell to Lagos, you know that you will always hold a piece of this megacity in your heart, forever changed by the lessons it has taught you and the memories it has given you. Lagos, with all its complexities and contradictions, will always be a part of your story.